# A TIME

## Robert G. Twycross
M.A., D.M., F.R.C.P.

Christian Medical Fellowship Publications
London

A Time to Die

An expansion of the annual
Rendle Short Lecture
given during the CMF National Conference, 1983

© Christian Medical Fellowship
157 Waterloo Road
London SE1 8XN

*First published* 1984

*Trade agents:*

*Inter-Varsity Press*
*Norton Street*
*Nottingham*

ISBN 0 906747 14 7

Photoset and printed in Great Britain by
Stanley L. Hunt (Printers) Ltd
Midland Road, Rushden, Northants

# A Time to Die

> 'For everything its season,
> and for every activity under heaven its time:
> A time to be born
> and a time to die' (Ecclesiastes 3:1-2).

Since 1971, I have been a full-time hospice doctor. My first five years were spent in London at St. Christopher's Hospice as Research Fellow in Therapeutics and at St. Joseph's Hospice as Visiting Medical Officer. Since 1976 I have been at Sir Michael Sobell House, a National Health Service hospice in Oxford. Sobell House has more than 100 patients on its register at any one time: 20 in-patients, 25 day patients and 60 out-patients. Each year some 400 terminally ill patients and families are cared for. It is necessary constantly to work from first principles in relation to symptom control. The psychological support of both patient and family is time-consuming and emotionally taxing. I am frequently asked by outsiders, 'How do you cope?' In part the answer is that the courage and fortitude of my patients and their families gives me a corresponding courage and fortitude to continue. This is made easier by the fact that it is always possible to relieve pain and other common symptoms considerably, if not completely, through a combination of drug and non-drug treatments. This means that I do not feel totally powerless even in the face of relentlessly progressive disease. But these are only part of the answer. In what follows I hope to examine from the doctor's point of view — and frequently from my own personal standpoint — some of the professional and emotional issues surrounding the care of dying patients.

**Man's common destiny**

Death — my death — is one of the few certainties in life. Yet at no time has Western man been less prepared to meet his appointed destiny. We live in a youth-oriented, health-worshipping, death-denying society. This means that death is 'all right' at arm's length — when it is in a book, on a film, in the news — but when it comes home to family, to place of work, to neighbour, that is an entirely different matter; we turn away, we cross the road, we pass by on the other side. Death denial is to a large extent consequent upon divorce from death. With a life expectancy of 70 years for males and 76 for females, only 7% of all deaths occur under 45 years of age. 60% of deaths are in the over-70 age group. A number of factors are responsible for improved life-expectancy. They include better perinatal and obstetric care, fewer deaths in childhood and from tuberculosis with the advent of antibiotics, encouragement of screening, higher safety standards at work and the absence of a major war for nearly 40 years. With the progressive move from village to town, to nuclear rather than extended families, we have to a great extent become divorced from death. So much so that, for example, a woman of 70 cannot face the death of her husband at home, and demands his admission to hospital, because she has never witnessed death or seen a corpse.

In such circumstances it is hardly surprising that our natural fear of death has become exaggerated. In the village, around the farmyard, half a century ago, things were different. There was a natural cycle of birth, life and death. The close-knit village community formed a natural, supportive extended family. Adults and children alike rubbed shoulders with death and, in so doing, kept the natural fear of death within bounds. Now, for many, divorce from death has resulted in an exaggerated fear coupled with unfamiliarity, awkwardness and embarrassment. Today's dying — and their fellow travellers, the bereaved — are today's lepers: unwanted, shunned, ignored.

It is important to recognize the natural tendency to withdraw from the dying, since doctors and nurses are not automatically immune.[1] To care successfully for the dying requires an initial determination to stay alongside, to visit regularly, and so to begin to meet the real needs of the stricken patient. It is not possible to train out all one's negative emotions for the fear of death is instinctive. It is part of the survival instinct. We all feel uneasy in life-threatening situations.

Unease is also felt in the presence of the dying because it evokes fear about one's own future death. In addition, there is a cultural factor: a collective fear of death. In every society, whether primitive or sophisticated, the corporate fear of death is focused on one or two particular diseases, or a group of diseases. In Europe and North America, cancer has taken over the role previously held by tuberculosis or, in generations past, by leprosy and plague. This has had the effect of making cancer more feared than almost any other disease — despite the fact that 30-40% of sufferers can now be cured. The popular image of cancer is not just negative, it is doubly so. The doctor's instinctive reaction to cancer is equally exaggerated. More than with most other diseases, a feeling of helplessness creeps in: 'There's nothing that I can do.'

Some of the doctor's emotional discomfort relates not just to existential anxiety, but to spiritual unease. We are all, to a greater or lesser extent, children of our generation. That is, we absorb the currently fashionable ideas and aspirations. These become our *raison d'être*. When confronted by death, our comfortable assumptions about life are often found wanting. The patient and his family ask: 'Why me?'; 'What have I done to deserve this?'; 'Where did I go wrong?' A naive belief that man is born with a guarantee of 'three score years and ten', that death is never today but always in the future, is seen to be without foundation. These questions, whether consciously or subconsciously, present themselves also to the doctor, who is forced to reconsider:

'Why am *I* here?'

'What am *I* really doing?'
'What is life all about?'
'What is the purpose of life?'
'What is the meaning of my existence?'
'What am I going to do with the rest of my life?'

Such questions inevitably force themselves into the mind. If the doctor cannot face up to them, anxiety will increase still further. Some doctors find themselves unable to care for dying patients at all. Others continue on only a very superficial level. Death is seen as the ultimate disaster, and terminal care a kind of macabre play in which the patient is 'jollied' along until the final curtain falls.

**The Lord of life and the fear of death**

St. Mark tells us how Jesus reacted when confronted with the fact that tomorrow he would die.

> 'When they reached a place called Gethsemane, Jesus said to his disciples, "Sit here while I pray." And he took Peter and James and John with him. Horror and dismay came over him, and he said to them, "My heart is ready to break with grief; stop here and stay awake." Then he went forward a little, threw himself on the ground, and prayed that, if it were possible, this hour might pass him by. "Abba, Father," he said, "all things are possible to thee; take this cup away from me. Yet not what I will, but what thou wilt." ' (Mark 14:32-36).*

---

* Scripture quotations are from the New English Bible, unless otherwise stated.

Up to this point, there had always been something between Jesus and his arrest, trial and death. The events of the previous week had been dramatically diverting: the triumphal entry into Jerusalem, the cleansing of the Temple, the verbal duals with the Pharisees, Herodians and Sadducees, the Last Supper. But now, there was nothing but a few hours of humiliation and torture between this man in the prime of life, at the peak of his power, and his death. Suddenly, with a rush, the reality of what is about to happen hits him with devastating starkness. And so we read that horror and dismay came over him, and he cried out: 'My heart is ready to break with grief. I cannot cope. I cannot take it. Abba, Father, get me out of this if you can.'

If it was like this for the Lord of Life, can we expect to fare any better? The stark reality was shattering, unnerving. He was temporarily panic-stricken as adrenaline surged through his body. 'In anguish of spirit he prayed the more urgently; and his sweat was like clots of blood falling to the ground' (Luke 22:44).

Yet St. John in his account tells us nothing of this. Instead we see Jesus in total command of the situation as he faces those who came to arrest him (John 18:4-8). The difference in emphasis possibly reflects the mood of the author. St. Mark, a teenager at the time of the Crucifixion, wrote his account under the direction of St. Peter just a few years after the events. Several decades later, St. John wrote as an old man waiting to be taken in death. The one young and vigorous like Jesus; the other in ripe old age — who might have said: 'My bags are packed and I am ready to go.'[2]

These observations confirm common experience. Facing up to the prospect of one's own death — not theoretically but in reality — is likely to be profoundly disturbing, at least at times, and particularly the night times. Nevertheless, given time, it *is* possible to adjust to one's approaching death to a greater or lesser extent. For those who reach grand old age adjustment is more likely to be a long drawn out process and may be relatively imperceptible.

Adjustment is not, however, simply an intellectual acceptance of a short life expectancy. It cannot be done in advance. The message must be modified: Yes, people can adjust; most people do cope — *when their time comes.* Moreover, in most diseases with a relatively well-defined terminal phase, adjustment is not a 'one off' event. Adjusting becomes a way of life as life becomes a series of losses: giving up physical recreation, premature retirement, inability to 'do-it-yourself' around the house, reduced social activities, diminished role in home management, giving up car-driving, use of wheelchair for daily 'walks', and so on. Each significant change requires acceptance and adjustment.

Canon David Watson, when he was ill with cancer, emphasized that the emotions take time to catch up with the intellect.[3] He identified, from a Christian perspective, the radical change that is necessary, from (intellectually) willing to be in heaven but (emotionally) wanting to be on earth to wanting to be in heaven but willing to stay on earth, until death comes.

David Watson also distinguished between the fear of death and the fear of the process of dying. At one time I would have denied that the two are essentially different. I now accept that in man, with his reflective mind, the two fears can be dissociated after the initial acute autonomic 'fight or flight' response has passed. I suspect, though, that for many, the dissociation is little more than an artifice to divert or distract the mind from the horror of death itself.

**Why me?**

The question 'why me?' (or its objective variant, 'why him?') is a near-universal response to a sudden marked change in fortune. It occurs when the change is dramatically for the better as well as for the worse. In the former, the good news largely palliates the emotional uncertainty. When the change is for the worse, the question is more persistent and more painful. The question 'why me?' still makes itself heard even through the intellectual awareness that most cancers are related to constitutional and environmental factors and not to lack of moral rectitude ('[God] makes his sun rise on good and bad alike, and sends the rain on the honest and the dishonest' (Matt. 5:45). It is an agonized cry for a listening ear, not a demand for a theological or philosophical answer.[4]

To respond intellectually is therefore not generally helpful. To be present, to listen, to empathize is what is called for: in silence maybe — or with an arm around the sobbing shoulder, a hug or embrace, a hand held. 'If I were in your position, I'd feel just as you do,' said quietly but sincerely. At the same time, one remembers (again most likely in silence) that, when ill and sick, there is only one place to look, and that is upwards. Prayer (again most likely in silence) can comfort but is no magic cure. Slowly, imperceptibly — not all at once — one seeks to help the sufferer move from why to what: what lessons about life can I learn from my predicament? 'At the important moments of life there are no answers, and it is more important to find a meaning.'

## On being angry with God

One of my former senior house physicians, now a general practitioner, wrote to me recently. He said: 'I have been in practice here for three years. I have looked after several dying patients at home since coming here: I find it extremely harrowing but very rewarding.' The last five words — *extremely harrowing but very rewarding* — describes succinctly the impact on the doctor of caring for dying patients.

Patients and families frequently express anger.[5] Doctors and nurses are inevitably called upon to 'soak up' other people's negative emotions and also to continue to cope with their own. The family's anger is often greater than the patient's. It is frequently accusatory, hinting at incompetence, and stresses that, in their opinion, I have failed.

What some patients and their families have to cope with seems so unfair. A mother of young children dying at 38 — A young woman of 23 fighting desperately for more time with her equally young husband, both shattered by the sudden death of a best friend from an intracranial haemorrhage — A man of 55, grandfather of two young children, whose father (the man's son-in-law) had died four years before in an accident. The first death adjusted to, but the children now being asked to face a second loss when still so young — A rapidly recurring sequence of illness, home-nursing, and death as parent followed by parent-in-law becomes ill. And now, when they had hoped for a few quiet years together, the husband or wife is discovered to have inoperable, end-stage cancer.

Also taxing, perhaps more so, are the extremes of unreality. Some hold so negative a view of cancer, that the patient is 'cursed' by fears and false anticipations. He fails to make use of the time that is left and hastens his death by increasing inanition and excessive fatalism. What a waste! And so annoying to those who would help make it *last* days rather than *lost* days. The other extreme is a total denial by the family of the fact that their loved one is now so limited in physical and emotional stamina that it is time to begin to let go. Instead 'He must get up' and the patient under duress says: 'Yes, I want another transfusion.' Flogging a dying horse is an apt description. How can they! So blind to reality, and so cruel. In addition, the negative emotions of bereavement;[6] in my case, occurring 400 times a year.

Coping with one's own and other people's negative emotions is one of the principal challenges of terminal care. Small amounts of negativity can be absorbed by most people, and coped with by 'evaporation' in the busyness of life. Larger quantities are dealt with through physical exertion — the long walk, jogging, gardening, and other absorbing hobbies. But there is a limit, above which neither 'evaporation' nor exertion suffices. Paul Tournier has written:[7]

> 'The phenomenon of the investment of violence [rage] and its transference from one object to another is to be found in many everyday situations. When an argument becomes heated, one of the participants will suddenly break off, saying, "I'm going for a walk to clear my mind!" He is investing in the effort of walking the violence he felt mounting within himself and which might have made him resort to blows. . . .'

> 'I have always been aware that my workshop provided a place where I could discharge my violence. Working on wood, steel, or gold, with hammer, saw, or file, I could invest the violence which my patients had poured out on me in the consulting-room. . . .'

> '[But my wife and I] often noticed that we had an argument every time that I had reconciled another couple. The couple had invested their violence in me, and I was investing it in my wife. . . .'

The same holds true for me. But is it right that my wife and children should be forced to absorb the excess negativity, as tiredness and stress lead inevitably to lost temper and angry words? An alternative method of emotional catharsis is clearly needed.

I turn to the Bible, to David's Psalms, and discover a principle that when emotionally shell-shocked by the battles of life, I should vent my frustration and anger on God. There are some who say: 'Oh no! we must never be angry with God.' For David, described as a man after God's own heart, and for me, there was and is no other way. I did not ask to be born. I did not ask to be a hospice doctor. I cannot cope with so much negativity. *Damn it, God, I cannot cope!* There is so much suffering, so much apparent unfairness. Yet on God's desk there is a framed statement. It says quite simply: the buck stops here. As someone said, 'If God had been Prime Minister, he would have been forced to resign aeons ago.'

Being angry with God is a necessity for me. Without this avenue of release, I could not continue as a hospice physician. I am still learning from David. Using his words to hang my anger on undoubtedly helps even though our circumstances are very different.

> 'Be gracious to me, O Lord, for I am in distress,
> and my eyes are dimmed with grief.
> My life is worn away with sorrow
>   and my years with sighing;
> Strong as I am, I stumble under my load of misery;
>   there is disease in all my bones.
> I have such enemies that all men scorn me;
>   my neighbours find me a burden,
>   my friends shudder at me;

> when they see me in the street they turn quickly away.
> I am forgotten, like a dead man out of mind.
> I have come to be like something lost'
> (Ps. 31:9-12).

The Psalms I find most helpful are those that express weariness of spirit as well as more obvious anger.[8] It is not just the former that I identify with: I need to be angry too. And to thank God that, in his infinite capacity to love and to give, he is able to absorb all my anger — and more.

**Professional friendship**

I recently attended a meeting at which speculations were made about the future of hospice care.[9] It was feared that the so-called Hospice Movement might end up merely as yet another technique to be added on to present-day high technology mainstream medicine — a technique behind which professionals could hide and through which they could soullessly exercise 'power'. The hope was expressed that this danger would be avoided, and that hospice care would continue to mean companionship — the friendship of professional staff with those who are dying.

In a crisis we all need friends. When dying we need a friend who can explain why there is pain, or shortness of breath, or constipation, or weakness, and so on. Someone who can explain what is happening in simple terms. Explanation is a key modality of treatment. It cuts the illness, and the symptoms, down in size psychologically. The situation is no longer shrouded in total mystery as there is someone who can explain what is going on. This is reassuring.

Other hospital staff sometimes comment: 'I suppose you become hardened to it in time and develop a protective shell.' The answer to that is an emphatic no. Obviously, one becomes more familiar with the many and varied practical challenges of terminal illness, and one acquires a certain confidence from this. But this is not the same as becoming hardened. For me, the opposite is true. I seem to feel more vulnerable as each year passes. Terminal care is, and ever will be, extremely demanding of the care-givers' emotional resources. I still find it hard to tell a patient; 'Yes it is a cancer'; 'Yes, the illness does seem to be winning.' It is especially hard if the patient is 16 or 26, though even at 76 or 86 it is never easy.

I have become more vulnerable as I try to offer more real and therefore more costly friendship. Dying is hard, and friendship with those who are dying is hard too. The demands are those laid on the disciples in the garden of Gethsemane: 'watch with me' (Mt. 26:38, R.S.V.). At the time of crisis I am asked to share the patient's mental suffering, and to feel naked and helpless in the face of death. If ever there comes a time when I find terminal care straightforward, that is a signal for me to leave medicine and take up market gardening. If ever it becomes easy, then I can be sure that I am no longer of any use to my patients.

## Care of the whole person

A hospice seeks to offer 'whole-person care'. The staff aim to help the patient to do his best given his personality, his family, his cultural background, his beliefs, his age, his illness, his symptoms, his anxieties, and his fears. There is need for flexibility. There is also a need to prevent that flexibility becoming an alternative rigidity. Unfortunately, this is an ever present danger as corporate man tends to take refuge in the 'comfort' of rules, regulations and routines. A freedom to invite patients to use Christian names can become oppressive if taken for granted. It is important to meet patients where they are psychologically and as they are physically and culturally. There is no such creature as the typical dying patient.

Body, mind, spirit and family relationships are all important. The patient and his family should be seen as the unit of care. There is much written about the physical and emotional needs of the dying; far less about spiritual care. Although perhaps harder to define and describe, the spiritual aspects of care are obviously important. In considering these, it is necessary to begin by asserting the obvious, namely, that man is a spiritual animal.[10] Human life is not simply governed by instinct. Human desire extends beyond the more fundamental appetites of food, comfort and sex. Man is a questioning and questing creature: 'Why, why, why?' Particularly when serious illness strikes, there is need to reflect on meaning and purpose in life. When newly released from concentration camp, Viktor Frankl wrote:[11]

'Another time we were at work in a trench. The dawn was gray around us; gray was the sky above; gray the snow in the pale light of dawn; gray the rags in which my fellow prisoners were clad, and gray their faces. . . . I was struggling to find the reason for my sufferings, my slow dying. In a last violent protest against the hopelessness of imminent death, I sensed my spirit piercing through the enveloping gloom. I felt it transcend that hopeless, meaningless world, and from somewhere I heard a victorious "Yes" in answer to my question of the existence of an ultimate purpose. At that moment a light was lit in a distant farmhouse, which stood on the horizon as if painted there, in the midst of the miserable gray of a dawning morning in Bavaria. "Et lux in tenebris lucet" — and the light shineth in the darkness.'

Frankl stresses an experience common to many who are trapped, whether by terminal illness or by political incarceration:

'The prisoner . . . experienced the beauty of art and nature as never before. . . . We were carried away by nature's beauty, which we had missed for so long.'[12]

Frankl also emphasizes that it is a peculiarity of man that he can live only by looking to the future — *sub specie aeternitatis.* Moreover:

'If there is a meaning in life at all, then there must be a meaning in suffering. Suffering is an ineradicable part of life, even as fate and death. Without suffering and human death, life cannot be complete.'[13]

And as Nietzsche said: 'He who has a *why* to live can bear almost any *how*.'[14]

The modern hospice is rooted in Christian philosophy, though in practice it is more broadly theistic. Those who work with the dying must believe in life, must believe that life is not just chance but design, and if design, then Designer. This is true whether expressed or not. Life is seen as having meaning and purpose throughout the period of dying. This conviction is manifested by attitudes and deeds rather than with words, and in how we respond to the dying and care for them, far more than in what we say. As always: actions speak louder than words. The unspoken message has been succinctly summarized by Dame Cicely Saunders:

> 'You matter because you are you.
> You matter to the last moment of your life,
> and we will do all we can
> not only to help you die peacefully,
> but to live until you die.'

It is this unspoken message that brings a sense of security to those we care for. And this security enables the individual patient to consider within himself those fundamental questions concerning life, God, and the hereafter. Such contemplation is greatly facilitated by the physical comfort for which hospices have rightly become noted.

Spiritual care is therefore basically non-verbal, but none the less real for that. Social workers and night nurses are perhaps most likely to receive overt spiritual questions. The Christian doctor is likely to find his main openings are with card-carrying Christians. It frequently surprises me how much help committed Christians need as their beliefs are forced to mature under the threat of impending death. Many Christians, like many non-believers, have a naive view of life and death. Christians have an added difficulty in that they often mistake emotional distress for lack of faith. I now expect my Christian patients to need more psychological support than the majority of others.

At Sir Michael Sobell House, we also have the services of the Hospital Chaplaincy and, of course, the patients' own clergy are welcome visitors. This provides one-to-one pastoral care as appropriate. Formal religious services are held twice a week for those who wish to attend. Almost more important are the prayers of many local well-wishers and of several convents in the vicinity of Oxford. In fact, I often feel that without the latter, our work would founder or grow stale.

**Euthanasia**

Although the literal meaning of the word euthanasia merely implies death without suffering, it is now generally defined as bringing about the death of a human being on purpose as part of the medical care being given him.[15] In relation to the terminally ill, a more precise definition is helpful — the administration of a drug (or drugs) deliberately and specifically to precipitate or accelerate death in order to terminate suffering. Euthanasia is incompatible with Christian belief.[15]

Time and again, those who thought that the choice lay between dying in agony and being killed have found an alternative in the hospice to which they have turned with enthusiasm. This is well illustrated in the following letter.[16]

The Producer                4 August, 1980
'World in Action'
Granada Television
Manchester

Dear Sir,

### World in Action 28.7.80

Having taken part in the making of the above programme I write to register my displeasure with the final product, which proved to be a biased and sensational platform for the pro-euthanasia lobby but gave little or no insight into the real plight of cancer patients, such as myself, and the viable alternatives to euthanasia which exist.

My cancer was diagnosed in November 1979 and my health deteriorated rapidly thereafter. By January of this year I was bedbound by pain and weakness, having been able to drink only water for six weeks. My wife has been told by our family doctor that I 'would die a painful death within three months'. I felt desperate, isolated and frightened and at that time I truly wished that euthanasia could have been administered. I now know that only my death is inevitable and since coming under the care of the Macmillan Service my pain has been relieved completely, my ability to enjoy life restored and my fears of an agonising end allayed. As you can see, I'm still alive today. My weight and strength have increased since treatment made it possible to eat normally and I feel that I'm living a full life, worth living. My wife and I have come to accept that I'm dying and we can now discuss it openly between ourselves and with the staff of the Macmillan Service, which does much to ease our anxieties.

My experiences have served to convince me that euthanasia, even if voluntary, is fundamentally wrong and I'm now staunchly against it on religious, moral, intellectual and spiritual grounds. My wife's views have changed similarly. I'm no longer in such misery that her love for me would make her want me to be dead. And after I've gone she will not have to fear the burden of guilt which would have been upon her had she wished for my early death. None of these feelings of mine were made clear to the viewing public in your programme which did nothing to shake the accepted view of cancer as a lingering, painful death, which can be avoided only by euthanasia. This lack of clarity was brought home to me when I was stopped in the street, by an inquisitor after the programme and asked 'was I for or against, after all?'

I agreed to take part in the making of your programme to show why I was against euthanasia; why it is wrong and how groups like the Macmillan Service can make it completely redundant. Truly I feel misrepresented and abused; and I am concerned that euthanasia, if fuelled by the media with sensation-seeking programmes such as yours, will become a reality and a final and irrevocable, ill-informed choice of frightened sufferers, who really need help to live, not to die.

>Yours faithfully,
>
>Sidney Cohen.

Consequently, as a practising physician, I find the very existence of the Voluntary Euthanasia Society anomalous. If a society to help the homeless was founded solely to campaign for the right of those without a home to opt for 'assisted suicide', few would consider it worthy of support, and many would seek to proscribe it on the ground that it would encourage some of the homeless to accept the option during a spell of transient depression or despair. Moreover, to limit a campaign to such an extreme solution would rightly be seen as casting a doubt on the wisdom, though not the sincerity, of the campaigners. As far as I am aware, no agency that is actively involved in caring for the disabled, the elderly or the terminally ill includes voluntary euthanasia among its aims.

I am reminded of the story told by Tolstoy of the death of Nicholas from tuberculosis in his novel *Anna Karenina*. Towards the end Nicholas is visited by his brother Levin and sister-in-law Kitty. The former is revolted by what he sees and finds himself powerless to do anything; but Kitty, with instinctive insight for what is needed, rolls up her sleeves and proceeds to wash, reclothe, make comfortable and feed the dying man.

For nearly 50 years, the Voluntary Euthanasia Society has sought to legalize voluntary euthanasia. One wonders what would have happened had its founder, Dr. Killick Millard, been like Kitty. One thing is certain; thousands of patients with terminal cancer would have had better care and pain relief than has been the case.

Having said that, however, I am the first to admit that there are still too many examples of abysmally poor care of patients dying of cancer. By means of post-bereavement visits to the surviving spouse of patients under 65 years of age, Parkes concluded that 20 per cent of cancer patients dying in hospital and almost a third of those dying at home do so with their 'severe and mostly continuous pain' unrelieved. In patients cared for at home, the main reason for poor pain control appeared to be a failure on the part of the general practitioner to ensure that regular doses of an appropriate analgesic were given in sufficient quantity to alleviate the pain.

However, the real reason is almost certainly more fundamental than this. A doctor who has not come to terms with the fact of his own future death will find it difficult to support the dying. One man of 54 became totally demoralized and for several months spent much of the time crying. He was so frightened that he clung to his wife and became 'hysterical' whenever she left the room. He received an injection each week and apparently was not able to go into hospital because a bed was not available. Similar accounts given by other respondents suggested that neurotic exaggeration was not the explanation. Several patients put up with their pain without complaint on the supposition that nothing could be done to relieve it or that their chances of recovery would be enhanced if they refrained from taking powerful analgesics.

A change in the law will not correct deficiencies in care. In fact, it is likely to make matters worse as it will remove the incentive for improvement. It would make it more likely that the patients would be offered the false choice of only two options – dying in agony and being killed. It would further reinforce negative attitudes towards dying and death and perpetuate the belief that death from cancer is inevitably a painful, sordid business. Although seemingly compassionate, in practice it would not be so. What is needed is not a change in the law but a change in emphasis in medical education, a greater realization by doctors of what can be done and a parallel determination to do it.

## The Christian perspective

The fact that we shall die causes us to reflect on life. If we believe that life originated in a chance occurrence millions of years ago, it is ultimately meaningless. Many Western writers and poets have stressed the futility of life without God. For example:

Samuel Becket: 'Life is an indefinite waiting for an explanation that never comes.'
Shakespeare: 'Life is a tale told by an idiot, full of sound and fury, signifying nothing.'
Longfellow: 'Life is but an empty dream.'

O'Henry: 'Life is made up of sobs, sniffles and smiles, with sniffles predominating.'

Ernest Hemingway: 'Life is just a dirty trick, a short journey from nothingness to nothingness.'

These men were honest — a mark of the poet, singer and thinker. They saw through the superficial and what they saw upset them. Life appeared futile. Though honest, they were shortsighted. The heart of the teaching of Jesus Christ is that this life is simply preparatory to the Real Life that comes after physical death. The world is a uterus and dying is the passageway to eternity.

Convinced Christians are, however, a minority group in Britain today. British culture is in many respects alien to Christian thought. It is neither natural nor easy to adhere to a Christian perspective. Thus the Christian has two general tasks: to recognize what is unhealthy in society from a psychosocial point of view and, at the same time, to learn the mind of Christ. I suggest the following steps:

1. *Hold a view of life which includes the fact of death*

Avoid a life perspective that is dependent on physical good health. It is necessary to see value in life for the handicapped, the disabled, the invalid and the elderly. De Gaulle was wrong when he said: 'Old age is a shipwreck.' For the Christian, *the best is yet to be.* It is this which gives meaning to every part of life, even in dementia, in dying and at the moment of death. When we begin to accept this Biblical perspective, we shall be better able to be supportive of the physically or mentally disadvantaged and the dying, for in them we shall see (by faith) meaning, indeed worth. Instead of being paralysed by negative pity we shall more easily offer empathic support.

## 2. *Associate with the dying and the disabled while still in good health*

This reinforces the fact that fullness of life is not dependent on physical health. Discover that, in sickness, life can take on new meaning. As one patient said: 'Dying makes life suddenly real.'

## 3. *Do not deny your human nature*

It is natural to fear death and the manner of our dying. When dying we tread unfamiliar territory. We are uncertain and unsure. Uncertainty causes anxiety. Anxiety easily leads to fear. A 37-year-old Christian doctor, dying from cancer, wrote:[17]

'Certainly the experience of dying is more difficult than I had expected.... [Adjustment] is a gradual process, but a very profound one.... There has to be an adjustment of roles within the family, particularly where the male partner is ill and he has been more dominant in decision-making. Arguments can easily arise, and trying to involve the husband may produce an outburst of frustration because he is unable to carry out his normal role. This increasing helplessness and dependence is more difficult for some people to accept than others. I found it very difficult.'

'As one grows weaker, shorter of breath, distended and uncomfortable, so living becomes more and more of an effort. It is hard not to grow selfish when the simplest matters become like a preparation for a twenty mile hill walk. Emotions are squeezed out like an empty toothpaste tube. There are no reserves left.'

'Against this background all but the greatest saints will become moody and irritable, making unkind or hurtful remarks to those they love most. Does he or she really understand what you, the patient, are actually going through? Possibly not, for it is certainly worse than I expected, and I have looked after many patients through terminal illness. But as a patient to a fellow patient, remember that your loved one is suffering as acutely as you are but in a different way, and following a path as lonely and desolate as your own.'

4. *Continued fear does not imply a lack of faith*
Genes, personality and family circumstances all play their part in determining whether peace or fear prevails. Most likely, both emotions will persist side by side. There is loneliness in dying even when surrounded by a loving family and friends. We all tend to fear loneliness. Thus, although the Christian should theoretically enjoy 'the peace of God which is beyond our utmost understanding' (Phil. 4:7), in practice this is not always so.

5. *Meditate on the teachings of Jesus Christ*
Jesus said:

'I am the resurrection and I am life' (John 11:25).
'There are many dwelling places in my Father's house; if it were not so I should have told you' (John 14:2).

These and other sayings leave us in no doubt as to our intended destiny. Not some hazy after-life but Real Life. The teaching of the New Testament is unequivocal: this life is the shadow, the solid is to come. Life on earth is merely preparation for life in eternity. Personally, I do not understand it. In fact, at times the thought appals me; it often scares me. But yet I accept it as true on the authority of Jesus Christ, who by his resurrection confirmed his claim to be, in a way I cannot comprehend, God incarnate.

As I meditate, I absorb. I begin to appreciate more deeply that Jesus offers me a new perspective in death as well as in life.

   Jesus Christ transforms life
   Jesus Christ transforms sickness
   Jesus Christ transforms persistent ill health
   Jesus Christ transforms old age
   Jesus Christ transforms death

The spectrum of hope no longer extends from hope of life to hope of a peaceful death. It extends further, to eternity through the certain hope of resurrection. Rendle Short believed this too and, when speaking of the certainty of life beyond the grave, often quoted this verse:

> 'Let us learn like a bird for a moment to take
> Sweet rest on a branch that is ready to break;
> She feels the branch tremble, yet gaily she sings.
> What is it to her? She has wings, she has wings.'

## References

[1] Hinton, J. (1972), *Dying* (second edition), Harmondsworth: Penguin Books.
[2] Words attributed to Pope John XXIII.
[3] Watson, David, BBC Radio, April 1983.
[4] Autton, N. Personal Communication.
[5] Kubler-Ross, E. (1970), *On Death and Dying*, London: Tavistock Publications.
[6] Parkes, C. M. (1975), *Bereavement. Studies of Grief in Adult Life*, Harmondsworth: Pelican Books.
[7] Tournier, P. (1978), *The Violence Inside*, London: S.C.M. Press, p. 71.
[8] Psalms 31, 39, 42, 43, 55, 69, 70, 73, 77, 88, 102, 142.
[9] O'Donovan, O. (1982), *Some Theological Questions about Death and Dying*, paper given February 1, 1982 to Oxford Field Group of Institute of Religion and Medicine.
[10] Hardy, A. (1979), *The Spiritual Nature of Man*, Oxford: Clarendon Press.
[11] Frankl, V. E. (1963), *Man's Search for Meaning*, New York: Pocket Books, p. 63.
[12] Ibidem, p. 62.
[13] Ibidem, p. 106.
[14] Nietzsche, quoted in Frankl, V.E., Ibidem, p. xi.
[15] *Euthanasia and clinical practice: trends, principles and alternatives* (1982), The Report of a working party. London: Linacre Centre.
[16] Cohen, S. (1980) in: *Macmillan Service, 5th Report*, London: St. Joseph's Hospice, p. 5.
[17] Casson, J. H. (1980), *Dying, The Greatest Adventure of my Life*, London: Christian Medical Fellowship, pp. 5, 10 and 12.

# Some C.M.F. Publications

---

*Also by Dr. Robert G. Twycross*

**The Dying Patient**  24pp  40p

---

**Dying: The Greatest Adventure of My Life**
James H. Casson  40pp  60p

**Respect for Life — A Symposium**  48pp  £1.25

**Suffering in Childhood**
Janet Goodall  24pp  75p

**God and the Handicapped Child — A Symposium**  52pp  £1.25

**The Influence of Christians in Medicine**
J. T. Aitken, H. W. C. Fuller and D. Johnson  196pp  £3.95

Publications list from:
C.M.F., 157 Waterloo Road, London SE1 8XN